D0629652

ILLUSTRATED SOCCER RULES

ILLUSTRATED SOCCER RULES

by
Jo Ann Ash Fairbanks

Johnny W. Welton, Ed.D., Editorial Director
John Davies, Technical Editor
Kerry Rotha, Illustrator

Contemporary Books, Inc.
Chicago

Library of Congress Cataloging in Publication Data

Fairbanks, JoAnn Ash.
   Illustrated soccer rules.

   Includes index.
   1. Soccer—Rules.   I. Rotha, Kerry.   II. Title.
GV943.4.F34   1983   796.334'02'022   83-1930
ISBN 0-8092-5520-0 (pbk.)

Books by Concepts Illustration Team
   Illustrated Soccer Rules
   Illustrated Softball Rules

Published by Contemporary Books, Inc.
180 North Michigan Avenue, Chicago, IL 60601
Manufactured in the United States of America
International Standard Book Number: 0-8092-5520-0

Published simultaneously in Canada by
Beaverbooks, Ltd.
150 Lesmill Road
Don Mills, Ontario M3B 2T5   Canada

Dedication

to **Jason,** my son, who introduced me to soccer;
to **Josh,** my son, who introduced me to coaching;
to **Roland Mares** who introduced me to playing soccer;

to **George Sharrard** and **Jerry Robinson,** my mentor assigners, who wisely guided me through those early years of game assignments and enabled me to "rise in the ranks" at just the right pace;

to **John Davies** for his caring instruction, capable technical advice, and continuing education;

to **Johnny Welton** for his vote of confidence in me as a knowledgeable (woman) official;

to **Sharon Welton,** his wife, my friend, who put up with both of us through it all . . .

and finally,
to my parents **Nicky** and **Joe Ash,** who just love me.

Jo Ann Ash Fairbanks

CONTENTS

New Rules

Section 1

Section 2

Section 3

Section 4

Section 5

Section 6

ILLUSTRATED SOCCER RULES

INTRODUCTION

Illustrated Soccer Rules is written from the belief that the laws of soccer are designed to bring enjoyment to the game for everyone — players, officials, and spectators alike. That enjoyment is increased by knowing the laws and most importantly by proper interpretation and application. The game of soccer, unlike most other sports, relies very heavily on the referee's judgment. This book is an attempt to help officials develop this judgment and to help players develop a better understanding of the laws and their application.

The book is organized into eight sections that cover the seventeen laws of soccer. Within each section, the illustrated text describes the most frequent situations, or plays that occur, each referenced by law number, paragraph, and section. For each play, the "Players" portion gives information on what the players may or may not do under the laws. The "Referee" portion describes what officials are required to do by law. A suggested sequence for performing these duties is also given and where possible, additional guidance is offered to aid the referee in those most difficult areas of officiating: interpretation and application of the laws.

Interpretation of the laws is of utmost importance in soccer, and I believe that ninety percent of soccer officiating involves individual referee judgment. Development of this sense of judgment comes

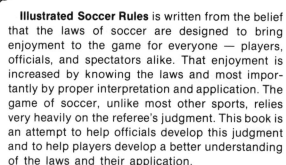

largely from experience, since each match is played with a different set of variables that impact a referee's decision. At all times an official must be acutely cognizant of the factors that influence how a game is to be officiated. Factors such as the age, skill level, experience, attitude, and size of the players must be considered by the official in making every decision. Other variables that also must be considered by the official before making a decision in a particular situation are competition level of the game, the score, cultural customs, language and gestures of the players, communication barriers, weather, and the behavior and attitude of spectators, team managers, and coaches.

While the circumstances under which a game is played may vary widely, perhaps the two most important factors that influence an official's interpretation of the laws are the age and experience of the players. With young and inexperienced players, an official must take special care in officiating the game. These players should first be *informed* (educated) about what they may or may not do under the laws. When an infringement occurs, these players should be informally *warned* on the first offense. A simple verbal comment such as, "You may not impede a goalkeeper from delivering the ball," will allow the wise player the space and humility to choose the correct behavior. The wording of the warning is the referee's choice, but might reflect those words in the "Players" portion of the plays contained here. Experienced or highly skilled players usually do not require a verbal warning, yet circumstances may determine whether the official will immediately penalize or choose to first give an informal, informational warning. Because these situations vary, I've addressed the problem in the text with the words, "Circumstances may require an informal warning." Astute, insightful recognition of those circumstances is a key to officiating soccer successfully. The other keys to success are referee knowledge of the laws, correct application of the laws, and professionalism.

It is my hope that **Illustrated Soccer Rules** will facilitate a greater understanding of the official laws, not only for players and officials, but for spectators, team managers, coaches, sponsors, and all people associated with the game. I've attempted to apply the meaning of the FIFA laws to those plays that most often occur in soccer and to explain the meaning (proper identification) in simple and direct language. In addition to the FIFA laws, there are local laws which may affect the official application in a particular match. It is important, therefore, for officials to be familiar with these local rules.

Application of the laws is partly a matter of an official's particular style. In applying the laws, I have used as my guideline the following maxim: Do as little as necessary to achieve players' and spectators' compliance with the laws. Even experienced and highly skilled players do not know the correct interpretation and application of the laws. It is beneficial to the game and the spirit of the laws for officials to give information to the players at appropriate times during the game. Often a simple statement will eliminate problems or confusion on the part of the players; for example, "You must remain ten yards from the ball until it has traveled its circumference."

To assist referees in applying the laws, the text uses two terms that distinguish between whether a free kick should be awarded or whether a player should be warned, cautioned, or ejected for infringements of the laws. The term "whistle the *play* dead" indicates that the ball was not in play, that is, not "alive," and therefore no free kick may be awarded. Players may only be warned, cautioned, or ejected in these dead ball situations. The term "whistle the *ball* dead" indicates that the ball was in play, or "alive," and free kicks can be awarded as well as any necessary warning, cautioning, or ejecting of players.

Professionalism in an official's appearance and demeanor in performing official duties cannot be overemphasized. Simply by dressing neatly, cleanly, and appropriately, and by acting with courtesy and consideration, an offical can earn the respect of all those associated with the game. I attribute what I call my success in soccer — meaning my enjoyment of the game as a player, coach, and offical — to the fact that I have learned and attempted at all times to treat all those involved with the game with respect and in a courteous and caring manner.

While this may appear self-evident, there are times when officials may feel offense toward players and spectators who harass them and question their decisions. Obviously, any retaliatory words or actions on the part of the official are inappropriate. Officials need to remember that in some sports (especially some American sports), officials are considered fair game and to harass them is "all part of the game." These people must be educated that those views and actions are not appropriate in soccer and officials play an important part in that acceptance and education.

The success of any soccer match can be measured by the enjoyment derived by the players, spectators, and officials. I believe that soccer is not just to be played, that the game is not just to be won — it's to be enjoyed. I hope that this book will provide a useful tool to all those who love the game.

Happy soccer!

Jo Ann Ash Fairbanks

4

Section 1

Laws I, II, III, and IV

**The Field of Play, the Ball,
Number of Players, and Equipment**

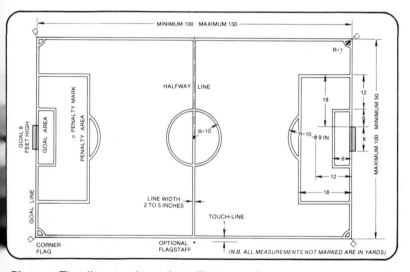

Players: The diagram shown here illustrates the correct measurements of the field and the accessories necessary for the game.

Referee: Often field measurements and conditions will vary, and usually there is little an official can do to remedy this. However, it is important for the official to pace off all the dimensions, check goal sizes, flag lengths, and net condition and attachment. Pay special attention to the center mark in the center circle and the penalty marks. Often holes occur at these places, and during the game players will try to place the ball elsewhere, which is not allowed.

   If these things are checked prior to the game, often game management can correct irregularities or unsafe conditions before play begins. Note any irregularities on the game card and report them to the appropriate authorities.

Reference: I

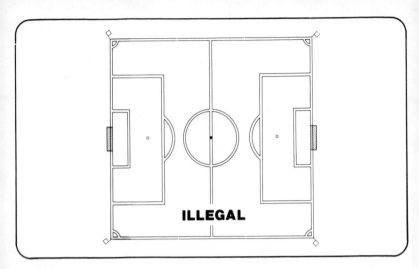

ILLEGAL

Players: The playing field is rectangular and the length must always exceed the width.

Referee: Note field irregularities on the game card and report them to the appropriate authorities.

Reference: I 1, IBD 1, 2.

Players: The playing field is to be marked with distinctive lines not to exceed five inches in width.

Referee: Distinguishing the field lines is often a problem. Cutting lines into the field should be discouraged since they can be dangerous to players and the ball can get trapped within the ridge of the cut line. Do not use lines that are less than two inches in width as they are difficult to see.

When line markings are questionable (or nonexistent), instruct players that you will whistle for out-of-play balls. Note irregularities on the game card.

Reference: I 2.

Players: A flag is placed at each corner of the playing field. The flag post must be no less than five feet high with a nonpointed top. (A similar flag may be posted not less than one yard outside the touchline at the halfway line).

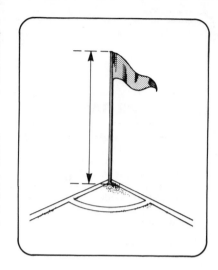

Referee: The flag post height is measured from the ground up; do not use the measurement of the post before it is installed. Remove a flag post that is less than five feet high as it presents a danger to players. Note such occurrences on the game card.

Reference: I.

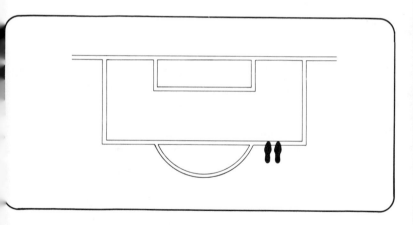

Players: The lines marking areas of the field are considered part of the area they designate.

Referee: A player standing on a line is considered to be inside the area the lines designate.

Reference: I IBD (6).

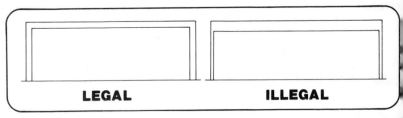

LEGAL　　　　　　**ILLEGAL**

Players: The width and depth of the goal posts and crossbar must not exceed five inches. The goal posts and crossbar must be the same width. The goal line is marked the same width as the depth of the goal posts and crossbar.

Referee: If irregularities in the goal posts or crossbar are dangerous to the players, correct the problem or abandon the game. Note the reason on the game card and report it to the appropriate authorities

Reference: I 6.

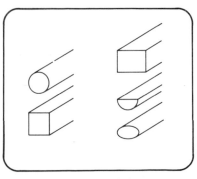

Players: Goal posts and crossbars must be made of approved materials (wood, metal) and may be round, rectangular, half-round, or elliptical.

Referee: Note irregularities on the game card and report them to the appropriate authorities.

Reference: I IBD (10).

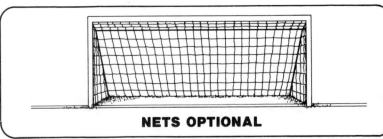

NETS OPTIONAL

Players: Nets may be attached to goal posts.

Referee: Local ruels may require the use of nets.

Reference: I.

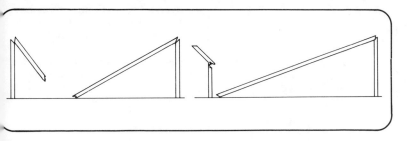

Players: Play is stopped when a goal post or crossbar is broken or dismantled during play.

Referee: Abandon the game unless the goal posts or crossbar can be repaired or replaced. Note the condition on the game card and report it to the appropriate authorities. If replacement or repair is accomplished, restart play with a drop ball at the place where the ball was when play was stopped.

Reference: I IBD (8).

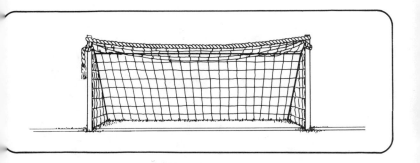

Players: A crossbar that is displaced or broken during a friendly game may be removed or replaced with a rope by mutual consent of the teams.

Referee: If it is decided that no rope or crossbar will be used, then your opinion determines when a goal is scored.

Reference: I IBD (8).

Players: The ball must be spherical and constructed of leather or other approved materials.

Referee: Examine and approve the ball. Look for protrusions or anything that may pose a danger to the players.

Reference: II.

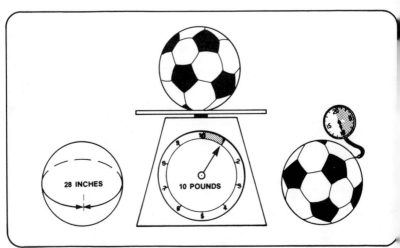

28 INCHES

10 POUNDS

Players: The ball must have a circumference of not more than 28 inches and not less than 27 inches. The weight of the ball at the start of the game should be no more than 16 ounces nor less than 14 ounces. The pressure of the ball should be from 9 to 10.5 pounds per square inch at sea level.

Referee: You do have the choice of accepting or rejecting a ball. When a ball becomes unsuitable during a game and is detrimental to the game or players, you may replace it.

Reference: II.

Players: The ball is returned to the referee at the end of the first half and at the end of the game.
Referee: Return the ball at the end of the game to the captain or coach of the team who owns it.
Reference: II IBD (1).

Players: A ball is replaced when it deflates or bursts during the game.
Referee: Whistle the ball dead. Examine and approve another ball. Restart play with a drop ball at the place where the ball became defective.
Reference: II IBD (4).

Players: Play is stopped when a ball becomes defective during a kickoff, goal kick, corner kick, free kick, penalty kick, or throw-in.
Referee: Whistle the play dead. Examine and approve another ball. Restart play with the throw-in or kick that was to be taken when the ball became defective.
Reference: II IBD (5).

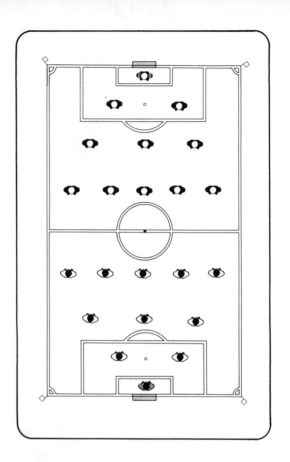

Players: A game is played by two teams, each having no more than eleven players on the field of play, one of whom must be a goalkeeper.

Referee: The minimum number of players required on the field varies according to local rules. FIFA recommends that a game played with teams of less than seven players should not be considered valid.

It is appropriate for a goalkeeper to participate outside of the penalty areas as a field player. However, a goalkeeper must be designated as such by each team.

Reference: III 1, IBD (1), (2).

Players: Substitutes may be used.

Referee: The number of substitutes allowed varies according to local rules.

Reference: III 2 (a), (b), (c), 3.

Players: Substitution may be made while play is stopped if the referee is informed of the substitution.

Referee: Whistle the play dead when a coach or player(s) requests a substitution. Call "Hold the Ball" for substitutions. Signal to restart play by whistling after the substitutions are made. Substitutions are completed when the players have left the field of play and the substitutes have entered the field.

Reference: III.

Players: Any player may change places with the goalkeeper while play is stopped if the referee is informed of the change.

Referee: Allow the change upon request only while the game is stopped.

Reference: III 4.

Players: If a player on the field exchanges places with the goalkeeper, play is not stopped.

Referee: Players and the goalkeeper must not exchange places unless there is a stoppage in the game and the referee is informed. If a violation occurs, allow play to continue until it has been stopped for another reason. Circumstances may require an informal warning. If not, caution the player and the goalkeeper as soon as the ball goes out of play or is whistled dead for another reason.

Reference: III 4, *Punishment* (a).

14

Players: Substitutes must await the referee's signal before entering the field, and they must wait until the players they are replacing have left the field. Substitutes must enter, and players must leave the field at the halfway line.

Referee: Players have a right to make substitutions, but be alert to abuses of this right. Substitution may be used as a device to delay the game, break down the play, or keep the score at a standstill. Therefore, the referee may deny substitutions if it appears that the stoppages are being used to gain an unfair advantage.

Players enter and leave at the halfway line in order to assure the proper number of players on the field.

Reference: III.

Players: The laws indicate that a player who is replaced by a substitute may no longer participate in the game.

Referee: Local rules may allow players to re-enter the game as substitute players.

Reference: III 5 (d).

15

Players: A substitute is subject to the authority of the referee whether or not the substitute participates as a player.

Referee: Substitutes may be dealt with in the same manner as players (either warned, cautioned, or ejected) as the infringement requires.

Reference: III 5 (e).

Players: Play is stopped when a substitute enters the field during play without permission of the referee.
Referee: Whistle the ball dead. Supervise the removal of the substitute from the field of play and either caution or eject the substitute from the game as circumstances require. Restart play by a drop ball at the place where the ball was when play was stopped.
Reference: III *Punishment* (b).

Players: A player who is ejected before the game starts may be replaced by a named substitute.

Referee: Supervise the removal of the ejected player. Allow a substitute to replace the player. Since time has not yet started officially, commence play with a kickoff. The ejected player may not participate in the game again.

Reference: III IBD 4.

Players: A player who is ejected after the game starts may not be replaced.

Referee: A team whose player is ejected must play one player short for the remainder of the game. Half-time is considered to be after the game has started and is under the jurisdiction of the referee. Therefore, a player may be cautioned or ejected during half-time. A team whose player has been ejected must play one player short in the second half.

Reference: III IBD 4; XII; V.

Players: A named substitute who is ejected before or after the game starts may not be replaced.

Referee: Ejection of a named substitute prior to the game usually means the player that the substitute is replacing is on the bench. The team would have eleven players on the field and one less substitute on the bench. When a substitute on the bench is ejected, another substitute may not replace the first one.

Reference: III IBD (4).

Players: No person may enter the field without permission of the referee.

Referee: Whistle the ball dead and stop play. Supervise the removal of the person from the field of play.

Persons entering the field can interfere with the game and could be injured. It is the referee's duty to preserve the players' enjoyment of the game and minimize interference from team doctors, managers, or spectators.

Reference: III 5 (c), IBD (8), (12) V (f).

Players: Play is stopped when a player or substitute enters the field of play without permission and commits a foul.

Referee: Whistle the ball dead. Circumstances may require an informal warning. If not, caution or eject the offending player and supervise the player's removal. Restart play with an indirect free kick for opponents at the place where the ball was when play was stopped.

Reference: III, *Punishment* (c); XII; V.

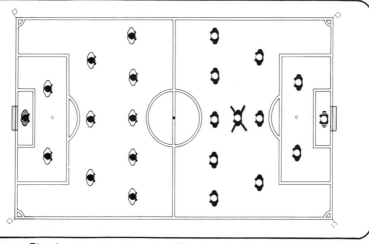

Players: Play is stopped when a twelfth player is discovered on the field during the course of play.

Referee: Whistle the ball dead. Supervise removal of the twelfth player. Restart play with a drop ball at the place where the ball was when play was stopped.

Reference: III 1.

19

Players: Play is stopped when a player requests the referee's permission to leave the field (usually for a minor injury) during the course of play and then plays the ball while leaving the field or does not leave the field.

Referee: Whistle the ball dead and caution the offending player as circumstances require. Restart play with an indirect free kick for opponents. Once a player requests and receives permission to leave the field during play, and there is no game stoppage, the player may not participate in the game until permission is received to re-enter the field.

Reference: III *Punishment (c).*

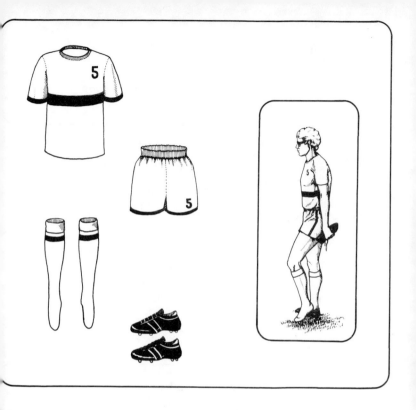

Players: Usual equipment for players is a jersey or shirt; shorts, a track suit, or similar pants; and socks and shoes.

Referee: While the law does not state that shoes are required, it could be unfair or dangerous for one or two players not to wear shoes when all the other players are wearing shoes.

Any article, such as a shoe, that comes off during play may not be carried in hand by a player. It could inadvertently become a weapon or be a danger to players. Tell the player to leave the field, replace the article, and return to play.

Players may wear track pants unless the rules of a specific match disallow this. Long pants must be disallowed if players use their protection to gain an unfair advantage (for example, dangerous slide tackling). This would also apply to knee pads, elbow pads, or other protective gear.

Reference: IV 1, IBD (1), (2), (3).

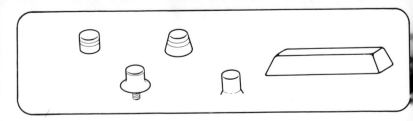

Players: Footgear must conform to the following description:

Bars can be made of leather or rubber and must run across the width of shoe and have rounded edges projecting not more than 3/4-inch. Individually placed studs may be made of leather, rubber, aluminum, plastic, or a similar material and must be solid, round, and no less than 1/2-inch in diameter (including tapered studs) and project no more than 3/4-inch. The screw in screw-in studs must be part of the stud.

No less than ten studs may be molded into the shoe and may be made of rubber, plastic, polyurethene, or a similar soft material. The studs must be no less than 3/8-inch wide and project no more than 3/4-inch.

Referee: Check the footgear of all players before the game begins. It is recommended that you feel screw-type cleats with your hand to detect rough edges which can tear the skin. These should be replaced or smoothed. Toe cleats are not allowed. Recheck the footgear of players who were requested to make adjustments.

Reference: IV 1, 2 (a), (b), (c), (d).

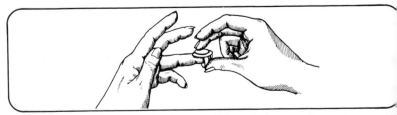

Players: Players may not wear anything that presents a danger to other players.

Referee: The referee, not the coach or players, determines what is dangerous to players. Check all players and substitutes before the game begins for equipment, clothing, or other articles that may endanger other players. Jewelry and hair ornaments, such as hairpins and plastic or metal ball bands, are often dangerous, if not to other players, then to the person wearing them. Instruct players to remove dangerous articles. Players refusing to comply should not be permitted to participate in the game.

Reference: IV 1, IBD (3), (4).

Players: The goalkeepers must wear colors which distinguish them from all other players and from the officials.

Referee: Make sure that the goalkeepers' uniform colors are distinct and easily recognizable from the players, goalkeepers, and officials. Allow goalkeepers to wear headgear if it is not dangerous or intimidating.

Reference: IV 1, 3, IBD (1), (4), (5), (6).

Players: Any player who has been prevented from playing or has been removed from the game because of improper equipment who reenters the game during play without reporting to the referee will receive a caution.

Referee: Whistle the ball dead and caution the offending player. Signal for an indirect free kick for opponents at the place where the ball was when play was stopped.

Reference: IV 1, IBD (5), (6).

Players: A player who is removed from the field and prevented from participating in the game because of improper equipment must report to the referee before re-entering the field.

Referee: Instruct the offending player to report to you for a safety check before re-entering the game.

Reference: IV 1, IBD (4), (5), (6).

Section 2

Laws V and VI

Referees and Linespeople

Players: The game must be officiated by a referee. The authority,
power, duties, and responsibili-
ties for administrating the game
commence when the referee
enters the field of play and ends
when the referee leaves the field
of play.

Referee: Entering the field of play
is interpreted here to mean the
vacinity of the playing area. You
do not have to step on the actual
field of play before authority
commences.

Reference: V; V IBD (1), (2), (3).

Players: A referee's decision is final. A referee may change a decision
only if play has not restarted.

Referee: It is inappropriate for coaches, players, or spectators to
attempt to sway an official's decision. If there is a change in decision
based on facts that the official did not have at the time of the original
decision, those facts may come only from official linespeople.

Reference: V; V IBD (5), (6), (11).

Players: The referee must keep a record of the game and act as time-keeper. The referee must allow the full or agreed time, adding time for injuries, time-wasting, or other causes.

Referee: The record is kept on an official game card, which is supplied by the presiding agency or a coach or manager. Promptly following the game, the referee returns the record to the presiding agency according to its rules.

The record of a game consists of cautions, ejections, which team scores, suspensions of the game for weather reasons, interference of spectators, misbehavior of coaches or other ancillary personnel, and field condition and markings.

In addition, referees should always maintain their own records of the games they officiate for licensing purposes and in case a more detailed report of a game is needed.

Reference: V (c), (d).

Players: The referee may terminate or suspend play for interference by weather, spectators, or other causes.

Referee: If weather conditions make play dangerous or take the enjoyment of the game away, either delay the game (if you think conditions may improve soon) or terminate it. The game may then be rescheduled. Consider the likelihood of play causing destruction to the field when you are thinking of terminating due to weather.

In the case of grave disorder, whistle the ball or play dead, leave the field immediately, and report the details as soon as possible to the appropriate authorities. Submit a written report as well. Under no circumstances does a referee, when terminating a game, determine which team wins. The referee only terminates the game; the appropriate authorities under whose jurisdiction the game was played determine what action is to be taken.

Reference: V (c), IBD (8), (9), (12).

Players: A game may be terminated by the referee before the time has run out due to inclement weather, spectator interference, or grave disorder.

Referee: Terminate the game and report the situation on the game card and to the authorities who will determine what action is to be taken.

Reference: V; VII.

Players: The referee will stop a game when serious injury occurs.

Referee: Whistle the ball dead and have the injured player removed by the appropriate personnel. Arrange for a substitute. Restart play with a drop ball at the place where the ball was when play was stopped. However, if you do not consider the injury serious, allow play to proceed. When the ball is out of play, delay the restart if necessary. Be aware that players may feign an injury in an attempt to get an official to stop play. Remember, players do have the option of kicking a ball out of play if they wish to stop play for the injury.

Reference: V (g), IBD (12).

Players: The referee has the power to stop play for infringements.

Referee: Whistle the play or ball dead for infringements and restart play as appropriate for the infringement. It is important to remember that it is at the referee's discretion to stop play or continue. Consider the intent, safety, enjoyment, fairness, level of play and the spirit of the game in deciding whether to stop or continue play.

Reference: V (d), (e), IBD (8).

Players: Free kicks are awarded to opponents of a team infringing the laws while the ball is in play.

Referee: Whistle the ball dead. Warn, caution, or eject the player(s) as the offense requires. Signal for the kick.

Reference: V; XII; XIII.

Players: Free kicks are not awarded to opponents of a team infringing the laws when the ball is out of play.
Referee: You may, however, caution or eject the offending player as circumstances require.
Reference: V; XII; XIII.

INDIRECT

DIRECT

Players: A player committing two infringements simultaneously or one immediately after the other is penalized for the more serious offense.
Referee: Whistle the play dead and signal for a direct free kick for opponents as the penalty for the more serious foul. Issue a caution if warranted.
Reference: V IBD (10); XII.

Players: Players and opponents may simultaneously foul each other while playing or attempting to play the ball.

Referee: Allow play to proceed as long as the simultaneous infringements are considered equal. However, if one player has taken unfair advantage over an opponent, whistle the ball dead. Signal for a direct or indirect free kick as required by the particular foul.

Reference: V (a), (d); VIII; XII.

Players: The referee has the discretionary power and the obligation to refrain from penalizing infringements when this may result in an advantage for the infringing team.

Referee: Signal and call "Play On" if you judge that playing the advantage is appropriate according to all aspects of the game. Do not stop play if doing so would give an unfair advantage to the infringing team. (Sometimes safety or the conduct of the players will make it unwise to play the advantage).

Depending on the level of play, you may allow the playing of advantage throughout the game or not at all. The playing of advantage does not preclude you from cautioning or ejecting the players later for the infringements. However, you may not reverse your decision if the presumed advantage is not realized.

It is best to try to have games played with as little interference from the referee as possible.

Reference: V (b), IBD (7), (8).

Players: A player may not attempt to impede the goalkeeper from putting the ball into play.

Referee: Whistle the ball dead. Signal for an indirect free kick and call "Impeding the Goalkeeper." Circumstances may require an informal warning with or without whistling the ball dead. If not, whistle the ball dead and caution the offending player. Then signal for an indirect free kick.

Reference: V IBD (8), (9).

Players: A referee will caution a player who is guilty of misconduct and unsportsmanlike conduct and will eject a player who is guilty of violent conduct, serious foul play, or the use of foul or abusive language.

Referee: If these infringements occur while the ball is in play, whistle the ball dead. Caution or eject the offending player as circumstances require. Restart play with a direct free kick for opponents if the infringement is one of the ten major fouls. Otherwise, restart play with an indirect free kick for opponents.

If the ball is out of play at the time of the infringement (such as for throw-in or goal kick), do not resume play until you have cautioned or ejected the offending player. Then restart play (with the throw-in or goal kick) as if the infringement had not occurred.

Reference: V (e), (h); XII.

Players: The referee will signal to restart play after play has been stopped.

Referee: The signal to restart play does not have to be a whistle. Avoid using the whistle except for "important" messages, such as for fouls, penalty kicks, kick-offs, doubtful situations when players are confused about starts and stops, start of the game, end of the game, and half-time. A corner kick may also need a whistle.

The verbal instruction, "Play On," accompanied by a wave of hand to restart play is sufficient. Some type of signal, however, is always required.

Reference: V (i).

Players: A game is restarted with a kickoff by opponents of the scoring team.

Referee: When assisted by official linespeople, verify that they both agree with the award of the goal before signaling. Then signal to center circle for a kickoff.

Reference: V; VIII (b).

Players: A ball is returned to the field of play by throwing it back in from the place where it left the field.

Referee: A throw-in may be taken one yard or so to either side of the place where the ball left the field of play. Do not allow players to gain yardage in either direction. When a player attempts or accomplishes this, whistle the play dead and have the player re-take the throw at the place where the ball left the field.

Reference: V; XV.

SIDE LINE

Players: A throw-in is taken by an opponent of the team which last played or had contact with the ball before it left the field of play over a touchline.

Referee: Signal which team is to take the throw-in by indicating the direction that team is traveling and call "Throw-in."

Reference: V (i); XV.

33

Players: An opponent may not impede or distract the player taking a throw-in by voice or action.

Referee: Whistle the play dead when a throw-in is impeded. Delay the throw-in before it is delivered. Circumstances may require an informal warning. Call "Play On." If the same player later repeats the offense, whistle the play dead, issue a caution, and call "Play On." Call "Retake" if the infringement occurs after the throw-in is delivered.

Reference: V; XV.

Players: The only duty of the club linespeople is to indicate when the ball is out of the field of play

Referee: The referee usually supplies the linespeople with flags so that they can perform their duties and instructs them regarding their duties.

Reference: VI.

Players: Two linespeople are appointed to assist the referee in administering the game.

Referee: The linespeople may be either two official linespeople who are referees serving as linespeople or two club linespeople who are associated with the teams.

Reference: VI; V IBD (5).

Players: Official linespeople assist the referee in controlling the game and communicate to the referee any infringements of the laws.

Referee: Instruct linespeople how and when you wish them to flag infringements of the laws. You decide what, if any, action should be taken based upon the linespeople's information. It is not appropriate for club linespeople to flag a player's misconduct or offside infringement.

Reference: VI IBD (1).

35

Players: A linesperson may be dismissed by the referee for inappropriate interference or improperties.

Referee: Give clear, concise, and thorough instructions to the linespeople to avoid difficulties. When an official linesperson's conduct requires a dismissal, file a complete report with the presiding authority for the game and with the association of the official.

Reference: VI.

Section 3

Law VII

Duration of the Game

Players: The duration of a game is two periods of 45 minutes each unless mutually agreed upon to be otherwise.

Referee: Leagues have the discretion to alter the length of the game. Coaches and referees have no authority to alter the duration of a game.

Reference: VII.

Players: Each half of a game is of equal duration.

Referee: If you discover that an error has shortened a period, return the players to the field to complete the period, if possible. Restart play by a drop ball at the place where the ball was when play was stopped. Indicate this occurrence on the game card.

Reference: VII.

Players: Allowances are made in each half of the game for time lost due to injury, timewasting, or other causes.

Referee: Stop your watch when a serious injury occurs that requires some time to deal with or when obvious timewasting is taking place. Stopping time is more expedient and accurate than adding time at the end of the half. Restart the clock when play resumes.

Reference: VII.

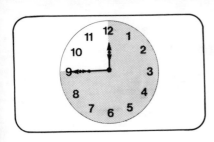

Players: Game time is extended in order to take a penalty kick if the kick was awarded before game time ran out.

Referee: Extend time for the penalty kick in the same half the penalty kick was awarded.

Reference: VII; XIV.

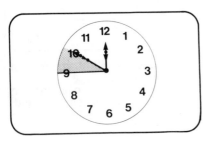

Players: The break between halves of the game (half-time) does not exceed five minutes unless altered by the referee.

Referee: The usual five-minute length of the half-time may be altered with your permission only.

Reference: VII.

Players: Players are entitled to a half-time.

Referee: Half-time must be provided even if only one player requests a half-time.

Reference: VII.

Section 4

Laws VIII, IX, and X

The Start of Play, Method of Scoring

Players: At the beginning of the game, team captains represent each team at the coin toss.

Referee: You may ask the home team captain to toss the coin while the visiting team captain calls "Heads" or "Tails." Many officials prefer to toss the coin themselves with the visiting team captain calling the toss while the coin is in the air.

Reference: VIII.

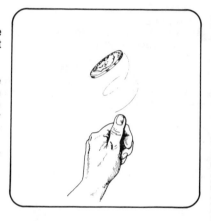

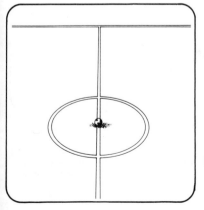

Players: A kickoff is taken at the designated spot in the center circle.

Referee: If the spot is not marked, the ball is placed on the halfway line in the center of the circle. Signal for the kickoff by whistling.

Reference: VIII.

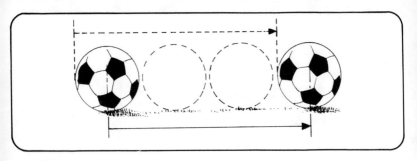

Players: On a kickoff, a ball is not in play until it has traveled its circumference.

Referee: Whistle the play dead when any player contacts the ball before it has traveled its circumference from the kickoff. Call "Retake." Then whistle for the retake.

If the kicker contacts the ball a second time, do not award an indirect free kick to the opponents since the ball was not in play when the second contact was made.

Reference: VIII.

Players: A kickoff by a person other than a player in the game does not officially start a game.

Referee: For ceremonial reasons, celebrities or persons not competing as players sometimes take a kickoff. Following the ceremonial kickoff, the game officially begins with a kickoff by participating players in the game.

Reference: VIII IBD (2).

Players: All players must be in their team's half of the field when the kickoff is taken and must remain there until the ball is in play.

Referee: Correct any player's position before signaling for the kickoff. Whistle the play dead if players move into the opponent's half during the kickoff. Call "Retake." Then whistle for the retake.

Reference: VIII.

Players: During the kickoff, opponents of the team taking the kickoff must remain outside the center circle (ten yards from the ball) until the ball is in play.

Referee: Delay the kick by calling "Hold the Ball" when opponents encroach within the center circle *before* the kickoff is taken. Whistle the play dead when opponents encroach within the center circle *during* the kickoff. Call "Retake." Then whistle for the retake.

Reference: VIII.

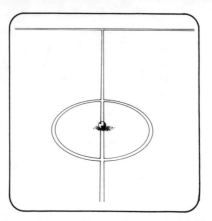

Players: The ball must be stationary for the kickoff.

Referee: Whistle the play dead if the ball is rolling when the kickoff is taken. Call "Retake." Then whistle for the retake.

Reference: VIII.

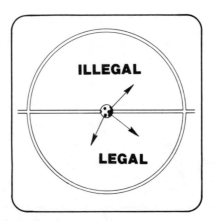

Players: The ball must be kicked forward into the opponents' half of the field at the kickoff.

Referee: Whistle the ball dead when the ball rolls along the halfway line or is kicked into the kicker's half of the field. Call "Retake." Then whistle for the retake.

Reference: VIII.

Players: A player taking a kickoff may not contact the ball again until it has been played by or made contact with another player.

Referee: Whistle the play dead when the kicker contacts the ball twice on the kickoff. Call "Playing the Ball Twice." Signal for an indirect free kick for the opponents after it is in play or signal for retake if the ball is not in play.

Reference: VIII.

Players: The team winning the coin toss has the choice of taking the kickoff or choosing which half of the field to defend.

Referee: Note on the game card which team takes the first kickoff to insure that the other team takes the kickoff at the beginning of the second half of the game. Make sure that the teams switch field ends before the start of the second half.

Reference: VIII.

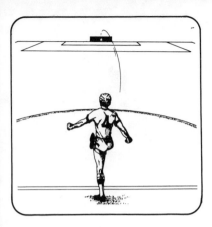

Players: A goal may not be scored directly from a kickoff.

Referee: Whistle the play dead when the ball enters the goal from a kickoff. Signal and call "Goal Kick."

Reference: VIII.

Players: The second half of the game starts with the opponents of the team who made the first kickoff of the game taking the starting kickoff. During the second half of the game, each team will defend the opposite side of the field that was defended in the first half.

Referee: Correct team positions if the teams take the wrong half of the field or if the wrong team prepares for the kickoff.

Reference: VIII (c).

Players: A drop ball is used to restart play when play is stopped for reasons not given in the laws.

Referee: Use a drop ball to restart play only in situations where the ball was in play at the time play was stopped. You may stand with a player from each team and call "Drop Ball" before dropping the ball. The ball is not in play until it touches the ground.

Reference: VIII (d).

Players: A drop ball is used to restart play when play is stopped for any cause not mentioned in the laws, such as for an injury not due to a foul.

Referee: Whistle the ball dead for serious or time-consuming injuries. Restart play by dropping the ball at the place where the ball was when play was stopped (not where the injured player was nor where the injury occurred). If a goalkeeper has possession of the ball, instruct him or her to release the ball. Then whistle the ball dead when, by the goalkeeper's delivery, it has reached a point closer to midfield. By allowing the goalkeeper to deliver the ball before stopping play, you avoid having to drop the ball in a goal or penalty area which would create an unfair advantage.

Reference: VIII.

Players: A free kick is not awarded if, when the referee drops the ball, any player infringes the laws before the drop ball is in play.

Referee: Whistle the play dead. Warn, caution, or eject the offending player as the infringement requires. Drop the ball again at the same place. No free kick is awarded to the opposing team because the ball was not yet in play at the time of the infringement.

Reference: VIII IBD (1).

Players: A drop ball is in play when it touches the ground.

Referee: Whistle the play dead when a player contacts the ball before it touches the ground. Call "Retake" and drop the ball again at the same place.

Reference: VIII (d).

Players: A drop ball is redropped if it goes over a touchline or goal line before making contact with a player.

Referee: Regain possession of the ball and drop it again at the site of the original drop.

Reference: VIII (d).

Players: The ball becomes dead when the referee stops play; it remains dead until the referee restarts play.

Referee: Whistle loudly enough for all players to hear you when you whistle for play to stop.

Reference: IX.

OUT   **IN**

Players: The position of the ball determines whether it is in play or dead, not the position of a person who is playing the ball.

Referee: Call "Play On" if players are confused about whether or not the ball is in play when the person playing the ball is outside the field of play.

Reference: IX.

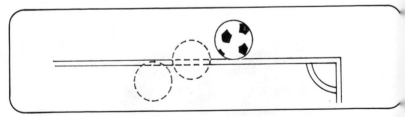

Players: A ball is in play if it is on a goal line or a touchline. The lines of the field are considered part of the field of play.

Referee: Call "Play On" when confusion results because of a ball being on a line.

Reference: IX IBD (1).

48

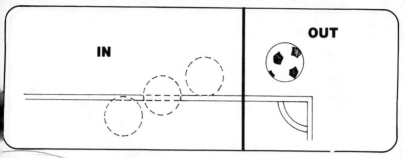

Players: The ball is dead when the entire ball has crossed an entire touchline or a goal line and is out of the field of play.

Referee: Whistle the play dead if the entire ball has left the field of play and the players have continued to play a dead ball. Call "Play On" if part of the ball remains on the field of play and the players are confused about whether or not the ball is in play.

Reference: IX IBD (1).

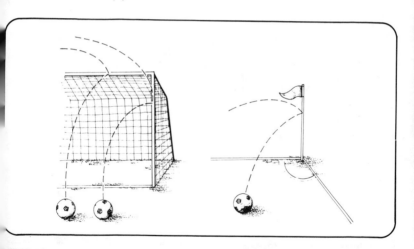

Players: The ball remains in play when it rebounds from a goal post, a corner flag, or a crossbar.

Referee: Call "Play On" if players are confused about whether or not the ball is in play.

Reference: IX.

Players: The ball remains in play when it rebounds off a referee or linesperson who is on the field of play.

Referee: Call "Play On" immediately if the ball strikes a linesperson or referee who is on or off the field if the ball itself does not entirely cross a field line. Players will often stop playing in these situations, so instruct them immediately to continue playing to keep the game moving.

Reference: IX.

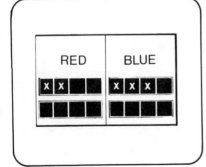

Players: The team scoring the most goals by the end of the game is the winner.

Referee: Note the scores or lack of scores for each team on the game card.

Reference: X.

Players: A game that ends with neither team scoring or each team scoring the same number of goals is a "Tie" or "Draw."

Referee: Note the scores or lack of scores for each team on the game card.

Reference: X.

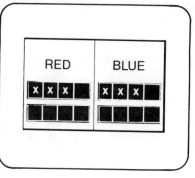

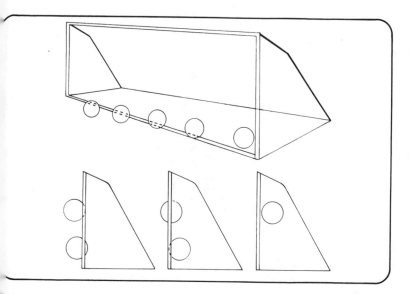

Players: A goal is scored when the entire ball completely crosses the goal line that is between the goal posts and under the crossbar.

Referee: When assisted by official linespeople, verify that the linesperson agrees with the award of the goal before signaling. Then signal to center circle for a kickoff.

Reference: X.

Players: A goalkeeper may score a goal by throwing the ball into the opponent's goal as long as the ball is thrown from within the goalkeeper's own penalty area.

Referee: When assisted by official linespeople, verify that the linespeople agree with the award of the goal before signaling. Then signal to center circle for a kickoff.

Reference: X.

Players: A drop ball is used to restart play when a spectator makes contact with the ball while it is in play.

Referee: Whistle the ball dead. Supervise the removal of the spectator from the field of play. Call "Drop Ball" and restart play by dropping the ball at the place where the contact occurred.

Reference: VIII; X IBD (2), (3).

Players: A goal is not scored when the ball is entering the goal and a spectator enters the field and makes contact with the ball or interferes with play.

Referee: Whistle the ball dead. Supervise the removal of the spectator from the field of play. Call "Drop Ball" and restart play by dropping the ball at the place where the interference occurred.

Reference: X IBD (3).

Players: The goal is considered scored when a ball is entering the goal and a spectator enters the field but does not make contact with the ball or interfere with play.

Referee: Signal for a kickoff after a goal is scored. Supervise the removal of the spectator from the field of play.

Reference: X; X IBD (2), (3).

Players: A goal is not scored if the ball is prevented from entering the goal due to contact with an outside agent, such as a spectator or a dog.

Referee: Whistle the play dead. Supervise the removal of the outside agent from the field of play. Call "Drop Ball" and restart play by dropping the ball at the place where contact occurred.

Reference: X; X IBD (2), (3).

Players: A goal is not scored when a player on the offensive team intentionally propels the ball into the goal by a hand or arm.
Referee: Whistle the ball dead. Signal for a direct free kick for opponents at the place where the infringement occurred and call "Hand Ball." If the infringement occurred in the goal area, the ball may be placed for the free kick anywhere within that half of the goal area where the infringement occurred.
Reference: X; XII.

Players: A goal is not scored from an indirect free kick when the ball goes directly into the opponents' goal.

Referee: Whistle the play dead and signal for a goal kick for opponents. No goal is awarded since the ball did not have contact with at least two players before entering the goal.

Reference: X; XIII.

Players: A goal is not scored from an indirect free kick when the ball goes directly into the kicker's goal.

Referee: Whistle the ball dead and signal for a corner kick for opponents.

Reference: X; XIII.

Players: A goal is not scored from a direct free kick when the ball goes directly into the kicker's goal.

Referee: Whistle the play dead and signal for a corner kick. A team may not score a goal against itself in this manner.

Reference: X; XIII.

Section 5

Law XI

Off-side

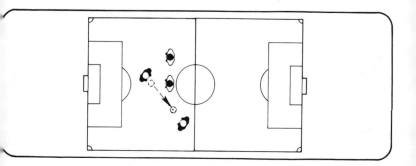

Players: All elements of the law are applied at the moment offside is judged.

Referee: If any one of the following elements does not exist at the moment offside is judged, the player cannot be declared offside. The must be in an offside position. The player must be nearer to the opponents' goal line than the ball is. The playere must be in the opponents' half of the field. There must be fewer than two opposing players nearer their goal line than the playere is. A player who is in an offside position is judged offside at the moment the ball is played by or makes contact with a teammate who plays the ball toward him or her. However, a playere who is in an offside position may not be declared offside if the playere is receiving the ball directly from a goal kick, a corner kick, a throw-in, or a drop ball from the referee. Additionally, a player who is in an offside position may not be declared offside unless the player is interferring with play, interferring with an opponent, or seeking to gain an advantage by being in that position.

Reference: XI.

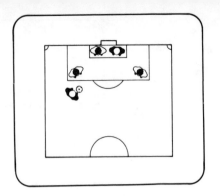

Players: A player is judged offside at the moment the ball is played or makes contact with a teammate.

Referee: This is the precise time to judge a player offside. A player cannot be declared offside if the player is ahead of the ball while both the player and the ball are in motion toward the opponents' goal. The ball must make contact with a teammate in order for a player who is in an offside position to be declared offside.

Reference: XI 2, IBD (1).

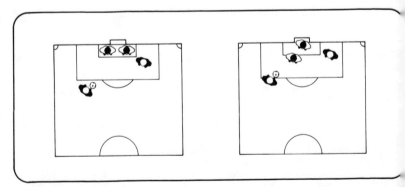

Players: A player cannot be declared offside unless the player is in an offside position.

Referee: When a player is not in an offside position at the moment the ball is played by a teammate, allow play to proceed.

Reference: XI.

Players: A player cannot be declared offside merely for being in an offside position.

Referee: Unless all the other elements apply to the player in the offside position, allow play to proceed.

Reference: XI 3.

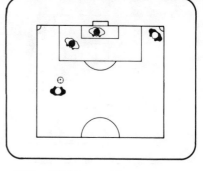

Players: Play is stopped when the referee declares a player to be offside.

Referee: Whistle the ball dead. Call "Offside" and signal for an indirect free kick for opponents.

Reference: XI 4; XIII.

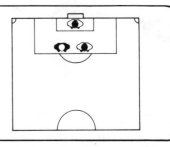

Players: A player is not in an offside position when two opponents are nearer to the goal line than he or she is.
Referee: Allow play to proceed.
Reference: XI 1 (b).

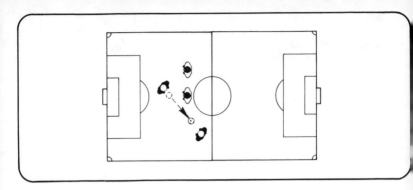

Players: A player is not in an offside position when positioned in the player's own half of the field.

Referee: Allow play to proceed.

Reference: XI 1 (a).

Players: A player in an offside position cannot be declared offside when that player receives the ball directly from a drop ball.

Referee: Allow play to proceed.

Reference: XI 3 (b).

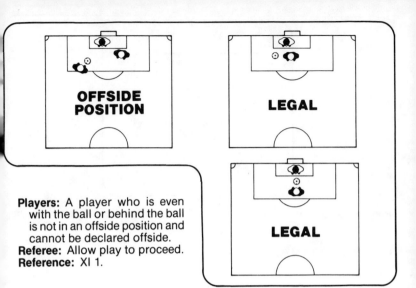

Players: A player who is even with the ball or behind the ball is not in an offside position and cannot be declared offside.
Referee: Allow play to proceed.
Reference: XI 1.

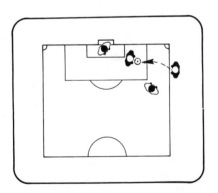

Players: A player in an offside position cannot be declared offside when receiving the ball directly from a throw-in.

Referee: Allow play to proceed.

Reference: XI 3 (b).

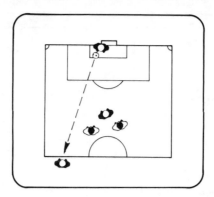

Players: A player in an offside position cannot be declared offside when receiving the ball directly from a goal kick.

Referee: Allow play to proceed.

Reference: XI 3 (b).

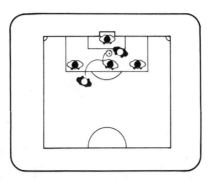

Players: A player in an offside position is declared offside when the ball is passed to the player from a teammate, even if the ball glances off of or is deflected by an opponent's body.

Referee: Whistle the ball dead. Signal for an indirect free kick for opponents and call "Offside." Offside is judged at the moment of the pass or shot to the player in an offside position; the ball's contact with the opponent's body occurred afterwards.

Reference: XI.

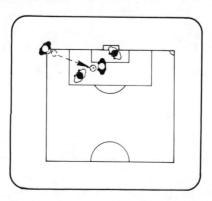

Players: A player in an offside position cannot be declared offside when receiving the ball directly from a corner kick.

Referee: Allow play to proceed.

Reference: XI 3 (b).

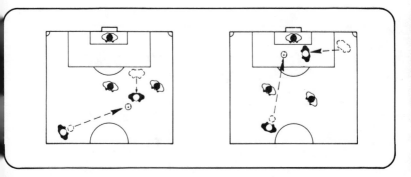

Players: A player is declared offside if he or she runs back from an offside position to play a ball that has been played forward by a teammate.

Referee: Whistle the ball dead. Signal for an indirect free kick for the opponents and call "Offside." Offside is judged at the moment the teammate plays the ball. By running back to play the ball, the player who was in the offside position was seeking to gain advantage from that position.

Reference: XI.

Players: A player in an offside position is not declared offside when a teammate is dribbling the ball toward the player.

Referee: Allow play to proceed. A player's offside position is judged at the moment the ball has contact with a teammate — if the teammate shoots, passes, or plays the ball to or toward that player. If a ball is being dribbled in a direction toward the offside player, this does not constitute a shot, pass, or play to that player.

Reference: XI 2, IBD (1).

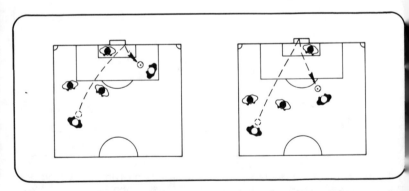

Players: A player in an offside position is declared offside if a teammate attempts a shot on the goal and the ball rebounds off a goal post or crossbar to the player in an offside position.

Referee: Whistle the ball dead. Signal for an indirect free kick for opponents and call "Offside."

Reference: XI.

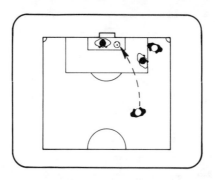

Players: A player in an offside position is declared offside if the referee judges that the player is interfering with play or with an opponent.

Referee: Whistle the ball dead. Signal for an indirect free kick for opponents and call "Offside." You may judge the player to be offside if, by any verbal or physical act, the player distracts or interferes with the opponent.

Reference: XI 2 (a).

Players: A player in an offside position is declared offside if the referee judges that the player is seeking to gain advantage by being in that position.

Referee: Whistle the ball dead. Signal for an indirect free kick for opponents and call "Offside."

Reference: XI 2 (b).

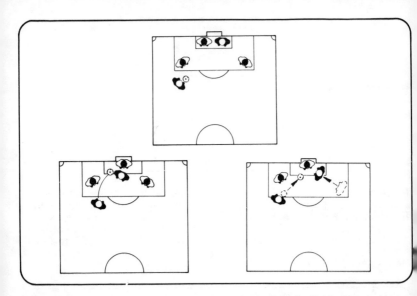

Players: A player in an offside position is declared offside if the player interferes with or obstructs the goalkeeper when the ball is played by a teammate.

Referee: Whistle the ball dead. Signal for an indirect free kick for opponents and call "Offside." Warn or caution the offending player. No goal may score.

Reference: XI.

Section 6
Law XII
Fouls and Misconduct

Players: A player may not impede an opponent's progress to the ball by interposing the body between the opponent and the ball.

Referee: Whistle the ball dead. Signal for an indirect free kick at the place of infringement and call "Obstruction." Often in obstruction fouls, no body contact is made by the player obstructing. If contact is made, it is usually made by the innocent player colliding with the obstructor. Caution is required to insure that the victim of the obstruction is not called for the forced collision with the obstructor.

Reference: XII 3.

Players: A player may not intentionally impede an opponent's movement with any part of the body.

Referee: Whistle the ball dead. Signal for a direct free kick and call "Holding." The hands, arms, legs, and body used in this manner is considered a holding foul.

Reference: XII (g).

Players: A player may screen the ball with the body while keeping the ball within playing distance as it proceeds toward and over a goal line or touchline.

Referee: A player screening the ball must keep the ball within playing distance. There is often a fine line between obstructing and screening in this particular situation, so you may need to take a clue from the body position and facial expressions of the screener.

Reference: XII IBD (7).

Players: A player may screen the ball with the body while keeping the ball within playing distance as it approaches the possession of the player's goalkeeper.
Referee: A player screening the ball must keep the ball within playing distance and be screening the ball with the body without obstructing an opponent. There is often a fine line between obstructing and screening in this particular play, so you may need to take a clue from the body position and facial expressions of the screener.
Reference: XII IBD (7).

Players: A player may charge an opponent when the opponent is screening the ball.

Referee: Allow play to proceed. The charge must be a fair charge; that is, contact must be made in the shoulder area and not in the spine.

Reference: XII (e), IBD (2).

Players: A player may not intentionally charge an opponent from behind.

Referee: Whistle the ball dead. Signal for a direct free kick and call "Charging." A deliberate and intentional charge warrants a caution. If the charge is violent or considered serious foul play, an ejection is warranted.

Reference: XII (e), (m), (n); V (d), (h).

Players: A player may not fair charge an opponent when the ball is not within the playing distance and the charging player is not attempting to play the ball.

Referee: Whistle the ball dead. Signal for an indirect free kick any call "Fair Charge for Not Playing the Ball."

Reference: XII 2.

Players: A player may fair charge the goalkeeper in the goal area.

Referee: If the goalkeeper is within his own goal-area, he may be charged only when he is in possession of the ball, or obstructs an opponent with the ball within playing distance. The charge shall be shoulder to shoulder and therefore, neither dangerous nor violent. If the goalkeeper is outside of his own goalarea, he may be charged fairly even though he is not in possession of the ball, but it must be within playing distance. (See note for youth soccer following.)

Reference: XII 4 (a).

Players: A player may not fair charge the goalkeeper in the goal area when the goalkeeper is not holding the ball.

Referee: Whistle the ball dead. Signal for an indirect free kick at the place of infringement and call "Charging the Goalkeeper."

Reference: XII 4 (a); V (i), IBD (3).

Players: A player may not fair charge the goalkeeper in the goal area unless the goalkeeper is obstructing the opponent.

Referee: Whistle the ball dead. Signal for an indirect free kick at the place of infringement and call "Charging the Goalkeeper." NOTE: In youth soccer, the goalkeeper cannot be charged in any manner in the penalty area or goal area. Therefore, a fair charge would call for an indirect free kick and a violent or dangerous charge or a charge from behind would require a direct free kick. Intentional and deliberate fouls warrant a least a caution.

Reference: XII 4 (b).

Players: A player may not kick or attempt to kick a ball held by the goalkeeper.
Referee: Whistle the ball dead. Signal for an indirect free kick for opponents and call "Dangerous Play." Circumstances may require an informal warning. If not, caution or eject the offending player as the infringement requires. An ejection is warranted if you judge the action to be serious foul play.
Reference: XII 1.

71

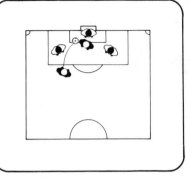

Players: A player may not obstruct the opponent's goalkeeper.

Referee: Whistle the ball dead. Signal for an indirect free kick for opponents and call "Obstructing the Goalkeeper." Warn or caution the offending player as circumstances require. No goal may score.

Reference: XII.

Players: The goalkeeper who has possession of the ball within the goalkeeper's own penalty area may take no more than four steps before releasing the ball into play.

Referee: Whistle the ball dead. Signal for an indirect free kick for opponents at the place where the fifth step occurred.

Allow the goalkeeper to gain control of the ball before counting steps. Allow the goalkeeper a reasonable time to make a decision about when, where, and how to release the ball. Whether the goalkeeper is bouncing the ball, throwing it in the air, or holding it, only four steps are allowed. Thereafter, the ball must be released.

A goalkeeper may stop the ball with the body and then foot-dribble the ball further out from the goal area before picking up the ball. Therefore, do not count steps until the goalkeeper takes hand control of the ball.

Reference: XII 5 (b).

Players: A goalkeeper, within the goalkeeper's own penalty area, who has gained control of the ball and then released it, may not have hand control of the ball again until it has been played by, or had contact with, another player.

Referee: Whistle the ball dead. Signal for an indirect free kick for opponents at the place where the contact occurred.

Rolling the ball on the ground is considered as having released the ball. The goalkeeper may, however, play the ball with the feet, head, or body.

Reference: XII 5 (a).

Players: A goalkeeper may not waste time by lying on the ball longer than necessary.

Referee: Whistle the ball dead, signal for an indirect free kick and call "Timewasting." Circumstances may require an informal warning. If not, caution the goalkeeper. Call this foul only when the goalkeeper is wasting time to gain an unfair advantage.

Reference: XII 5 (b), IBD (12).

Players: A player may not jump at an opponent.

Referee: Whistle the ball dead. Signal for a direct free kick at place of infringement and call "Jumping At." Circumstances may require an informal warning. A deliberate and intentional foul warrents at least a caution. If the foul is violent or considered to be serious foul play, an ejection is warranted.

Reference: XII (c), 1, (n); V (e), (h).

Players: A player many not kick, strike, trip, push, spit at, or use foul or abusive language toward teammates.

Referee: Consider playing the advantage prior to stopping play in the ball is out of bounds and/or dead to caution or eject the offending player as circumstances require. If play is stopped to administer a caution or an ejection, signal for an indirect free kick at the place of infringement. While teammates cannot technically foul each other, unsportsmanlike conduct of this nature should not be tolerated.

Reference: XII (m), (n), (o), (last paragraph); V (b), (d), (e), (h), IBD (4), (7).

Players: A player may not intentionally kick or attempt to kick an opponent.

Referee: Whistle the ball dead. Signal for a direct free kick at the place of infringement and call "Kicking" or "Attempted Kick." A deliberate and intentional kick warrants at least a caution. If the kick is violent or considered to serious foul play, an ejection is warranted.

Reference: XII (f), (n); V (d), (e), (h).

Players: A player may not intentionally trip or attempt to trip an opponent.

Referee: Whistle the ball dead. Signal for a direct free kick at the place of infringement and call "Tripping" or "Attempted Trip." A deliberate and intentional trip warrants at least a caution. If the trip is violent or considered to be serious foul play, an ejection is warranted.

Reference: XII (b), (m), (n); V (e), (h).

Players: A player may not intentionally form a "back" or "bridge" to trip or attempt to trip an opponent.

Referee: Whistle the ball dead. Signal for a direct free kick at the place of infringement and call "Tripping" or "Attempted Trip." A deliberate and intentional trip warrants at least a caution. If the trip is violent or considered to be serious foul play, an ejection is warranted.

Reference: XII (b), (m), (n); V (e), (h).

75

Players: A player may not intentionally charge an opponent in a violent or dangerous manner.

Referee: Whistle the ball dead. Signal for a direct free kick at the place of infringement and call "Charging." An intentional charge of this nature warrants at least a caution. If the charge is violent or considered to be serious foul play, an ejection is warranted.

Reference: XII (e), (m), (n); V (e), (h).

Players: A player may not intentionally strike or attempt to strike an opponent.

Referee: Whistle the ball dead. Signal for a direct free kick at the place of infringement and call "Striking" or "Attempted Strike." A deliberate and intentional strike warrants at least a caution. If the strike is violent or considered to be serious foul play, an ejection is warranted.

Reference: XII (f), (m), (n), IBD (13); V (d), (e), (h).

Players: A player may not spit at an opponent.

Referee: Whistle the ball dead. Signal for a direct free kick at the place of infringement and call "Spitting." Spitting is considered to be a form of striking and warrants an ejection.

Reference: XII (F), (m), (n), IBD (13), V (d), (e), (h).

Players: A goalkeeper may not throw or attempt to throw the ball at an opponent.

Referee: Whistle the play dead. Signal for a direct free kick and call "Striking." If the goalkeeper commits or initiates the strike from within the penalty area, signal for a penalty kick. Give the signal even if the opposing player is outside of the penalty area when the strike or attempted strike is made. If the goalkeeper attempts to strike an opponent with the ball, at least a caution is warranted. If the ball makes contact with the player, an ejection is warranted.

Reference: XII (f), (m), (n); V (d), (e), (h), IBD (1).

Players: A player may not push an opponent.

Referee: Whistle the ball dead. Signal for a direct free kick at the place of infringement and call "Pushing." A deliberate and intentional push warrants at least a caution. If the push is violent, an ejection is warranted.

Reference: XII (f), (h), (m), (n); V (d), (e), (h), IBD (4).

Players: A player may not intentionally handle the ball with a hand or arm.

Referee: Whistle the ball dead. Signal for a direct free kick and call "Hand Ball." Caution the offending player for unsportsmanlike conduct if the foul is committed intentionally, especially if done to stop the ball from entering the goal. What determines a hand ball foul is whether the player's hand or arm moves to contact the ball. If the ball merely strikes the hand or arm without this type of movement by the player, the contact is not considered a hand ball foul.

Reference: XII (i), (m); V (d), (e).

Players: A player may not play the ball with a high kick in close proximity to an opponent when it creates a danger to the opponent.

Referee: Whistle the ball dead. Signal for an indirect free kick for opponents and call "Dangerous Play." A high kick is usually higher than waist level and should be called only if it is dangerous to an opponent.

Reference: XII 1.

Players: A player may not play the ball with a low head close to an opponent when it creates a danger.

Referee: Whistle the ball dead. Signal for an indirect free kick and call "Dangerous Play." Usually a low head is at waist level or below. Stop play when a player in this position creates a danger by being near an opponent who is attempting to kick the ball.

Reference: XII 1.

Section 7

Laws XIII and XIV

Free Kick and Penalty kick

Players: Play is stopped when a player is inadvertently put in a position of bodily danger.

Referee: Whistle the ball dead. Restart play with a drop ball at the place where the ball was when play was stopped. If the player deliberately puts himself or herself in a dangerous position (for example, by intentionally falling on the ball), this is considered an infringement. Whistle the ball dead. Signal of an indirect free kick and call "Dangerous Play."

Reference: XII 1, 3, IBD (7).

Players: There are two types of free kicks; direct, from which a goal may be scored directly, and indirect, from which a goal is scored only if the ball has last been played or had contact with any two players.

Referee: Always signal an indirect free kick by raising an arm straight above your head. Maintain that position until the ball makes contact with a player other than the kicker, or goes out of the field of play. After whistling the ball dead for an

infringement, signal which team is to take a direct free kick by raising your arm for a few seconds to a 45-degree angle in the direction that team is going. You may also call color of the team to take the free kick.

Reference: XIII; XIII IBD (1).

Players: Opponents of a player taking an indirect free kick from inside the kicker's penalty area must remain at least ten yards from the ball outside the penalty area until the ball is in play.

Referee: Delay the kick by calling "Hold the Ball" when opponents are within ten yards of the ball before the kick is taken. Pace off ten yards from the ball and indicate the position the players should take. Signal for the kick to be taken by whistling when the opponents have complied.

Reference: XIII.

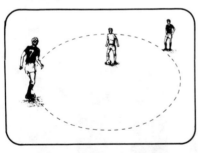

Players: Opponents of a player taking a free kick must remain at least ten yards from the ball until the ball is in play.

Referee: Allow play to proceed when the kicker chooses to take the free kick with opponents less than ten yards from the ball. (The kicker may have more advantage than if the opponents were ten yards from the ball and the kicker was required to delay.)

Instruct opponents to move the ten-yard distance when the kicker waits for them to move ten yards from the ball and they have not done so. Signal for the kick to be taken by whistling when the opponents have complied.

Always signal for a free kick to be taken. When the kicker chooses to take the quick free kick, the signal may be simultaneous with the kick.

Reference: XIII.

Players: Free kicks must be taken from the place where the infringement or foul occurred.

Referee: Incicate the location of the infringement by pointing when the ball is not placed at the appropriate position for coverage of the next play. While the ball should be placed at the site of the infringement, a location within a yard or so of the exact spot is considered appropriate.

Reference: XIII.

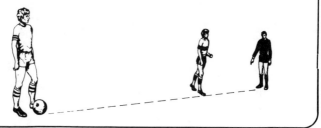

Players: A player taking a free kick may ask the referee to enforce the ten-yard distance requirement.

Referee: Delay the kick by calling ' Hold the Ball" when the kicker asks to have the ten-yard distance requirement enforced. Pace ten yards from the ball and indicate the position the opponents should take. Signal for the kick to be taken by whistling when the opponents have complied.

Reference: XIII.

Players: Opponents of a player taking a free kick may be less than ten yards from the ball within their penalty area only if they are on the goal line between the posts.

Referee: If an indirect free kick is taken within less than ten yards of the goal, the opponents may be less than ten yards from the ball if they are on the goal line between the posts. Opponents not standing on the goal line between the posts must be ten yards away from the ball for the free kick.

Reference: XIII.

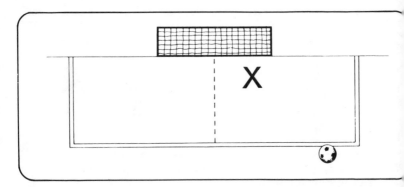

Players: Free kicks to be taken in the kicker's goal area may be taken anywhere in that half of the goal area in which the infringement occurred.

Referee: Unlike all other free kicks, those taken in a kicker's goal area need not be placed at the site of the infringement.

Reference: XIII.

Players: Opponents of a player taking a free kick from inside the kicker's penalty area must be at least ten yards from the ball and outside the penalty area until the ball is in play and outside the penalty area.

Referee: Delay the kick by calling "Hold the Ball" when opponents encroach within the kicker's penalty area before the kick is taken. Instruct the opponents to leave the penalty area. Signal for the kick to be taken when they have complied.

Whistle the play dead when opponents encroach within ten yards of the ball or into the penalty area during the kick. Instruct the opponents to leave the penalty area and call "Retake."

Allow play to proceed when opponents of the kicker are leaving the penalty area and attempting to comply with the law and the kicker chooses to take a quick free kick.

Reference: XIII.

Players: Opponents may not intimidate or distract, through voice or action, a player taking a free kick.

Referee: Whistle the ball dead when the kick has been taken and you judge that playing the advantage is not appropriate. Circumstances may require an informal warning. If not, caution or eject the offending player as circumstances require. Signal for an indirect free kick for the opponents.

   Whistle the play dead when the kick has not been taken. Call "Hold the Ball." Warn or caution the offending player as circumstances require. Signal for an indirect free kick to be taken.

Reference: XIII; XII; V.

Players: The ball must be stationary when taking a free kick.

Referee: Whistle the play dead when a free kick is taken with a moving ball. Call "Retake."

Reference: XIII.

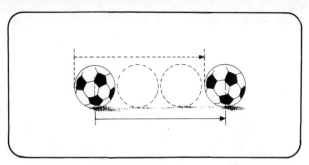

Players: On a free kick, the ball is not in play until it has traveled its circumference.

Referee: Whistle the play dead when a player contacts the ball before it has traveled its circumference from the point of the free kick. Call "Retake" and signal for the kick to be taken.

Reference: XIII.

Players: The ball is not in play until it has left the penalty area of the kicker who is taking a free kick.

Referee: Whistle the play dead when the kicker plays the ball a second time or another player contacts the ball before it has left the penalty area. Call "Retake" and signal for the kick to be retaken.

Reference: XIII.

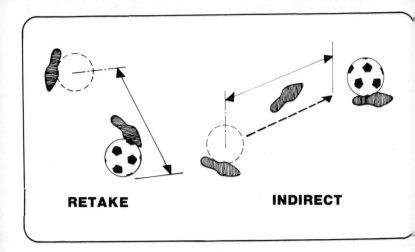

RETAKE

INDIRECT

Players: A player taking a free kick may not play the ball again until it has been played by or made contact with another player.

Referee: Whistle the ball dead. Signal for an indirect free kick for opponents if the ball traveled its circumference before the kicker played the second time. Call "Playing the Ball Twice." Call "Retake" if the ball did not travel its circumference before the kicker played it the second time.

Reference: XIII.

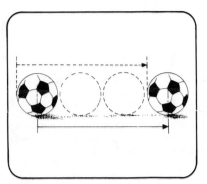

Players: On a penalty kick, a ball is not in play until it has traveled its circumference forward.

Referee: Whistle the play dead when a player contacts the ball before it has traveled its circumference forward. Call "Retake."

Reference: XIV.

Players: A penalty kick is retaken when opponents encroach on a penalty kick.
Referee: Whistle the ball dead. Call "Retake." Signal for the penalty kick by whistling.
Reference: XIV.

Players: Penalty kicks must be taken at the penalty mark.
Referee: If the penalty mark is not present, the ball is placed 12 yards from the goal line to a point equidistant between the goal posts. Indicate the spot to the kicker by pointing.
Reference: XIV.

Players: The opposing goalkeeper of a player taking a penalty kick must stand on the goal line between the goal posts without moving the feet until the ball is kicked.

Referee: Instruct the goalkeeper of these requirements prior to signaling for the penalty kick. A swaying movement from side to side by the goalkeeper is allowed, but any forward movement of the goalkeeper's feet off the line is an infringement. If an infringement occurs and the ball goes in to the goal, award the score. If the ball does not go in to the goal, the penalty kick is retaken.

Reference: XIV.

Players: A player taking a penalty kick may not contact the ball again until it has been played by or made contact with another player.

Referee: Whistle the ball dead when kicker contacts the ball twice on a penalty kick. Signal for an indirect free kick for opponents and call "Playing the Ball Twice."

Reference: XIV.

Players: A player taking a penalty kick must kick the ball forward.

Referee: Whistle the play dead when a player does not play the ball forward. Call "Retake."

Reference: XIV.

Players: A goal may be scored directly from a penalty kick.

Referee: When assisted by official linespeople, verify that the linesperson agrees with the award of the goal before signaling. Then signal to center circle for a kickoff.

Reference: XIV.

Players: Play is stopped when a ball from a penalty kick rebounds into play from a goal post or crossbar and makes contact with an outside agent.

Referee: Whistle the play dead. Supervise the removal of the outside agent and call "Drop Ball." Drop the ball at the place where contact occurred.

Reference: XIV IBD (b).

Players: Game time is extended for the taking of a penalty kick if it was awarded before game time ran out.

Referee: Extended time for the penalty kick. Whistle the ball dead and the end of half or end of the game when the goal is scored; the goalkeeper stops or catches the ball; the ball rebounds into the playing field from the goalkeeper, goal posts or crossbar; or the ball leaves the field of play.

Reference: XIV.

Players: When opponents of a player taking a penalty kick infringe after the signal it given, the penalty kick is retaken if a goal is not scored.

Referee: Whistle the ball dead when opponents of the kicker infringe and a goal is not scored. Circumstances may require an informal warning. If not, caution the infringing player. Then signal for a penalty kick and call "Retake."

Reference: XIV (a).

Players: When teammates of a player taking a penalty kick infringe after the signal is given, the kick will be taken if a goal is not scored, whether the ball returns into play, goes out of play, or is carried over the goal line by the goalkeeper, an indirect free kick will be awarded.

Referee: Whistle the ball dead when teammates of the kicker infringe and a goal is not scored. Circumstances may require an informal warning. If not, caution the infringing player. Then signal for an indirect free kick for opponents.

Reference: XIV.

Players: A player taking a penalty kick may not feign the kick in order to get the goalkeeper to move.

Referee: Whistle the play dead. Circumstances may require an informal warning. If not, caution the infringing player. Then signal for a penalty kick and call "Retake." (A free kick is not awarded since the infringement occurred before the ball was in play.)

Reference: XIV.

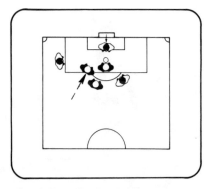

Players: When the goalkeeper moves and an opponent encroaches simultaneously on a penalty kick, play is stopped whether or not the ball enters the goal or returns to the field of play.

Referee: Whistle the play dead. Signal for a penalty kick and call "Retake."

Reference: XIV.

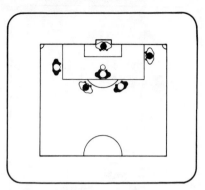

Players: All players except the kicker taking the penalty kick and the opposing goalkeeper must be and remain outside the penalty area at least ten yards from the penalty mark but within the field of play until the ball has been kicked.

Referee: Delay the kick by calling "Hold the Ball" when players encroach within ten yards of the penalty mark or into the penalty area before the kick is taken. Instruct the players to leave the penalty area and penalty arch. Signal for the kick to be taken when all players have complied.

Reference: XIV; XIV IBD (1).

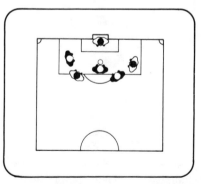

Players: Play is stopped when players of both teams encroach into the penalty area or penalty arch during a penalty kick, whether or not the ball goes into the goal or returns to the field of play.

Referee: Whistle the play dead. Signal for a penalty kick and call "Retake."

Reference: XIV.

KICKING TWICE

Players: A goal is not scored when a player taking a penalty kick infringes.

Referee: Whistle the play dead and signal for an indirect free kick for opponents. Circumstances may require an informal warning to the infringing player.

Reference: XIV (c).

Players: When teammates of a player taking a penalty kick infringe after the signal is given, the penalty kick is retaken, when the ball enters the goal.

Referee: Whistle the play dead. Signal for a penalty kick and call "Retake." Circumstances may require an informal warning to the infringing player.

Reference: XIV (b).

Players: When opponents of a player taking a penalty kick infringe after the signal is given and the ball enters the goal, the goal is scored.
Referee: Delay your call until the kick is completed. If the ball enters the goal, award the goal.
Reference: XIV.

Players: A penalty kick is retaken when the ball is prevented by an outside agent from entering the goal after the kicker has taken a penalty kick.
Referee: Whistle the play dead. Supervise the removal of the outside agent. Signal for a penalty kick and call "Retake."
Reference: XIV, XIV IBD (2) (a).

Section 8
Laws XV and XVII
Throw-in and Corner Kick

Players: The player taking a throw-in must face the field of play when releasing the ball

Referee: It is inappropriate to whistle the play dead when the thrower is not directly facing the field of play. A throw-in is simply a means of returning the ball into play.

Reference: XV.

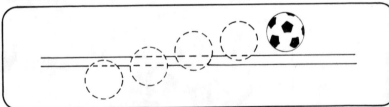

Players: A throw-in is taken when the whole ball completely crosses a touchline and is therefore out of play.

Referee: Whistle the play dead only when the players have continued to play a ball which is out of the field of play. If the ball is on the touchline, call "Play On." This call eliminates doubt as to the status of the ball and keeps the game moving. This also helps preclude a player from handling the ball while it is still in the field of play

Reference: XV.

Players: The player taking a throw-in must have part of both feet on the ground at the moment the ball is released.

Referee: Whistle the play dead when a player delivers the ball with only one foot or neither foot touching the ground. Signal for opponents to take the throw-in and call "Foul Throw." NOTE: Demonstrate with your foot the illegal action of the thrower to communicate to players and spectators the specifics of the infringement.

Reference: XV.

Players: The player taking a throw-in may have one foot or part of both feet on the touchline or outside the field of play at the moment the ball is delivered.

Referee: Whistle the play dead when the thrower takes the throw-in on the field of play. Call "Foul Throw" and signal for opponents to take the throw-in.

Reference: XV (a).

ILLEGAL

LEGAL

Players: A player taking a throw-in must use both hands to deliver the ball.

Referee: Whistle the play dead for an illegal delivery. Call "Foul Throw" and signal for opponents to take the throw-in. A spin on the ball does not necessarily mean the ball was delivered with one hand. Monitor the hands and body of the thrower, not the spin on the ball. Watch for the player who appears to be throwing the ball with both hands but is actually supporting the ball with one hand and throwing with the other hand.

Reference: XV (a).

Players: A player taking a throw-in must throw the ball from behind and over the head.

Referee: Whistle the play dead for an illegal delivery. Call "Foul Throw" and signal for opponents to take the throw-in. If a player's face is turned to the side when delivery takes place, allow play to proceed.

Reference: XV (a).

Players: A ball is considered to be in play the moment it enters the field of play on a throw-in.

Referee: When the ball crosses part or all of the touchline and immediately leaves the field of play, whistle the play dead. The ball is considered to have entered and left the field of play. Signal for opponents to take the throw-in and call "Throw-in."

Reference: XV.

Players: A throw-in that is delivered but never enters the field of play is retaken by the same team.
Referee: Whistle the play dead and call "Retake."
Reference: XV.

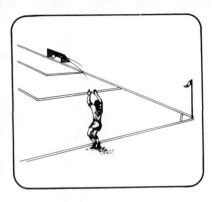

Players: A goal may not be scored directly from a throw-in.

Referee: Whistle the play dead when the ball is thrown directly into the goal. Signal and call "Goal Kick" if thrown into opponents goal or "Corner Kick" if thrown into own goal.

Reference: XV.

Players: A player taking a throw-in may not contact the ball again until it has been played by or made contact with another player.

Referee: Whistle the ball dead when the thrower contacts the ball twice on a throw-in. Call "Playing the Ball Twice" and signal for an indirect free kick for opponents.

Reference: XV (b).

Players: A thrower may not handle the ball with a hand or arm after completing a throw-in.

Referee: Whistle the ball dead and signal for a direct free kick for opponents.

Reference: XB IBD (1).

Players: A player taking a throw-in may not throw the ball at an an opponent for tactical reasons.

Referee: Whistle the ball dead. Circumstances may require an informal warning. If not, caution the player for unsportsmanlike conduct. Then signal for an indirect free kick for opponents. If the infringement is done as a "strike," whistle the ball dead. Eject the player for violent conduct and signal for a direct free kick for opponents.

Reference: XV; XII; V.

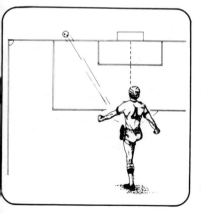

Players: A goal kick is taken when the ball leaves the field of play over a goal line when the ball last made contact with an offensive player.

Referee: Signal for a goal kick and call "Goal Kick." Indicate the side of the goal area from which the kick is to be taken. Whistle the play dead for a goal kick only if there is some confusion on the part of the players as to whether the ball is off the field of play.

Reference: XVI.

Players: A goal kick is taken by an opponent of the offensive team that last played or had contact with the ball before it crossed the goal line and left the field of play.

Referee: Advise players as to which team should take the goal kick if confusion occures.

Reference: XVI.

Players: Opponents of a player taking a goal kick must remain outside the penalty-area until the ball leaves the penalty area and the player taking the goal kick or a teammate may not play or have contact whith the ball until it reaches a point beyond the penalty area.

Referee: Instruct the opponents to move outside the penalty area. Whistle the ball dead when a player contacts the ball before it is beyond the penalty area. Signal for a goal kick and call "Retake."

Reference: XVI, IBD (1).

Players: A player taking a goal kick may not contact the ball again until it has been played by or made contact with another player.

Referee: Whistle the ball dead when the kicker contacts the ball twice on a goal kick. If the second contact by the kicker is within the penalty-area, signal for a goal kick and call "Retake." If the second contact by the kicker is beyond the penalty-area, signal for an indirect free kick by the opponents and call "Playing the Ball Twice."

Reference: XIV, IBD (1).

Players: A corner kick is taken when the ball leaves the field of play over a goal line when it last made contact with a defensive player.

Referee: Signal for a corner kick and call "Corner Kick." Indicate the corner from which the kick is to be taken. Whistle the play dead for a corner kick only if there is some confusion on the part of the players as to whether the ball is off the field of play.

Reference: XVII.

Players: A corner kick is taken by an opponent of the team that last played or had contact with the ball before it crossed the goal line and left the field of play.

Referee: Advise player as to which team should take the corner kick if confusion occurs.

Reference: XVII.

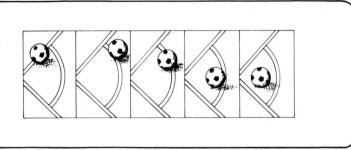

Players: The ball must be placed entirely within the quarter circle for the corner kick.

Referee: Whistle the play dead when the ball is not entirely placed within the quarter circle. Have the ball properly placed and signal for the corner kick to be taken.

Reference: XVII.

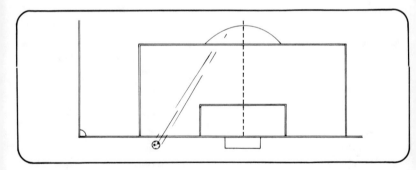

Players: A corner kick is taken from the quarter circle closest to the location where the ball left the field of play.

Referee: Whistle the play dead when the players proceed toward or place the ball at the improper corner. Signal by pointing to the proper corner.

Reference: XVII.

Players: The corner flag may not be removed or adjusted in order to take a corner kick.

Referee: Whistle the play dead if a player removes or attempts to adjust the flag. Supervise the repositioning of the flag and call "Retake."

Reference: XVII.

Players: Opponents of a player taking a corner kick must remain ten yards from the ball until the ball is in play.

Referee: Signal for the kick to be taken when the opponents have complied with the ten-yard distance requirement.

Reference: XVII.

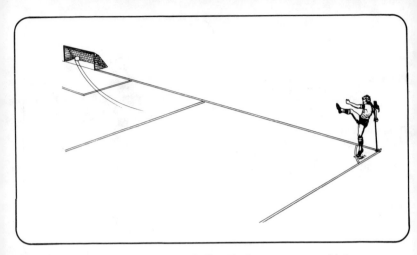

Players: A goal may be scored directly from a corner kick.

Referee: When assisted by official linespeople, verify that the linesperson agrees with the award of the goal before signaling. Then signal to center circle for a kickoff.

Reference: XVII.

Players: A player taking a corner kick may not contact the ball again until it has been played by or made contact with another player.

Referee: Whistle the ball dead when the kicker contacts the ball twice on a corner kick. Signal for an indirect free kick for opponents and call "Playing the Ball Twice."

Reference: XVII.

GLOSSARY

Caution: A formal, official acknowledgment of a serious infringement, conveyed by displaying the yellow card.

Defensive Team: The defending team, or the team without possession of the ball.

Deliberate and Intentional: Any illegal action that is committed for a purpose and has been deliberately planned.

Ejection: A formal, official acknowledgment of a serious infringement, conveyed by displaying the red card. The ejected player must leave the field and premises and may no longer participate in the game.

Encroachment: An illegal movement of an opponent into an area or within the required ten-yard distance before or during free kicks, goal kicks, penalty kicks, corner kicks, or kickoffs.

Fair Charge: A charge in which the player has arms and hands against the body and nonviolently "charges" into the shoulder area of the opponent. A charge into the spine or chest of an opponent is not considered a fair charge.

Goalkeeper Possession: Secure control of the ball by the goalkeeper, usually when the goalkeeper has hand(s), arm(s), or body over the ball.

Hand Ball: An illegal movement when the hand intentionally moves toward and makes contact with the ball. A movement of the ball toward a hand that makes contact is not considered a hand ball foul.

In Play: The time when the ball is considered alive and the only time in which free kicks may be awarded for infringements of the laws.

Into Touch: The situation when the ball passes outside of the field of play and crosses a touchline.

Law XVIII: An unwritten, unofficial law usually referred to as the "Common Sense Law."

Obstruction: An illegal maneuver wherein a player prevents an opponent from playing or approaching the ball by positioning the body so that it serves as an obstruction in the path of the opponent. The difference between obstruction and screening is that obstruction is "playing the player" and screening is "playing the ball." (See Screening.)

Offensive Team: The attacking team, or the team in possession of the ball.

Outside Agent: Any object, animal, or person on the field of play when the ball is in play. Referees, linespeople, players, and substitutes are not considered outside agents.

Pitch: The field of play.

Place Kick: A kickoff.

"Quick" Free Kick: A free kick taken before opponents comply with the ten-yard distance requirement. The team taking the quick free kick may have the advantage, since opponents do not have time to set up their best defensive positions.

Sanctioned: A term used in the language of the laws to indicate penalization.

Screening: A legal maneuver wherein a player within playing distance of the ball protects the ball from an opponent by using the body as a screen between the opponent and the ball in order to retain control or team possession of the ball. The difference between screening and obstruction is that screening is "playing the ball" and obstruction is "playing the player." (See Obstruction.)

Serious Foul Play: Any illegal conduct of a violent nature, such as intentionally fouling opponents. Serious foul play is most often committed during the course of play. (See Violent Conduct.)

Spirit of the Game: The philosophy which allows all to enjoy the game of soccer with an understanding that participation can occur in a safe, enjoyable atmosphere without undue concern for one's safety or size and in an atmosphere of good sportsmanship.

Unsportsmanlike (Ungentlemanly) Conduct: Any conduct, verbal or physical, that infringes the laws or spirit of the game.

Violent Conduct: Any illegal conduct of a violent nature, such as striking or spitting at referees, linespeople, opponents, or teammates. Violent conduct is often committed by a player who is not really attempting to play the game. (See Serious Foul Play.)

Wall: A defensive position in free-kick situations consisting of two or more opponents standing side-by-side (legally, ten yards from the ball.)

Warning: An informal verbal comment by the referee to a player for less serious infringements.

Whistle Ball/Play Dead: An instruction to the referee to stop play by whistling.

REFEREE SIGNALS

Play On: Extend both arms forward and parallel to indicate that play is to continue despite an infringement.

Goal Kick: Point the arm towards the goal area from which the kick is to be taken.

Penalty Kick: Point the arm towards the penalty mark.

Indirect Free Kick: Extend the arm above the head. Maintain the signal until the kick has been taken and the ball has contact with another player or leaves the field of play.

Direct Free Kick: Point the arm in the direction where the kick is to be taken. The signal need not be maintained since it is solely a communication signal.

Corner Kick: Point the arm towards the corner from which the kick is to be taken.

Caution or Ejection: Display the yellow card for a caution and the red card for an ejection. Approach the player before showing the card and stand just beyond an arm's length from the player. Tell the player that you are cautioning or ejecting him or her and give the reason. For a caution, advise the player that the next card, whether for a cautionable offense or not, must be a red card. Record the name of the player, jersey number, team number, time of carding, and the reason for the caution or ejection. Ejections also require an additional expulsion report.

INDEX

INDEX